Drawing, Sketching and Cartooning

TECHNIQUES FOR DRAWING PEOPLE, PLACES, PETS AND CARTOON CHARACTERS

Copyright © QED Publishing, Inc 2006

First published in the UK in 2004 by
QED Publishing
A Quarto Group Company
226 City Road
London EC1V 2TT
www.qed-publishing.co.uk

Reprinted in this format 2006

A catalogue record for this book is available from
the British Library

ISBN 1-84538-577-2

Written by Deri Robbins
Designed by Wladek Szechter/Louise Morley
Edited by Sian Morgan/Matthew Harvey
Illustrated by Melanie Grimshaw

Creative Director: Zeta Davies
Senior Editor: Hannah Ray

Picture Credits
Corbis Rune Hellestad p15
Jean Coppendale p26, p28

Printed and bound in China

The words in **bold** are
explained in the Glossary
on pages 56 and 57.

Contents

coloured pencils

Tools and materials for sketching and drawing

Anyone can draw – it's just a matter of learning how to look at things! This book has lots of techniques to help you improve your drawings.

To get started, you'll need some art kit. Start with a pad of paper, a couple of pencils and a pencil sharpener. As you learn more, you might want to try some of the materials below.

Pencils

You need at least three types of pencil: 2H (a hard pencil, for sharp lines and details), **HB** (medium hard, for sketching) and 2**B** (a soft pencil, for drawing guide lines and for **shading**). 4B to 9B pencils are very soft, and are for dark shading.

Rubber

Not just for rubbing out: you can use it to make **highlights** in your drawings by revealing the paper.

Charcoal and chalk

Charcoal and **chalk** are great for quick sketches, for large areas of colour and for adding **texture**.

Chalk or oil pastels

Chalk pastels are soft and crumbly, and give a delicate, blurry effect when you smudge them. Oil pastels make brighter, stronger colours.

Pens and felt-tip pens

These are perfect for strong black lines or sharp detail. The **nibs** come in many different sizes – you need some thick and some thin ones.

Wax crayons

Cheap and good for making bold, colourful pictures and **resist work.**

Paper

Use lots of different types, sizes and colours of paper. You can make your own cheap sketchbooks by simply stapling scrap paper together. Save your best paper for your final drawings. Experiment with paper with different surfaces: smooth **cartridge paper** is best for pencil and pen drawings.

The rough surface of **sugar paper** is ideal for pastels, chalk, crayons and charcoal. The marks on the paper will look different depending on what sort of paper you use.

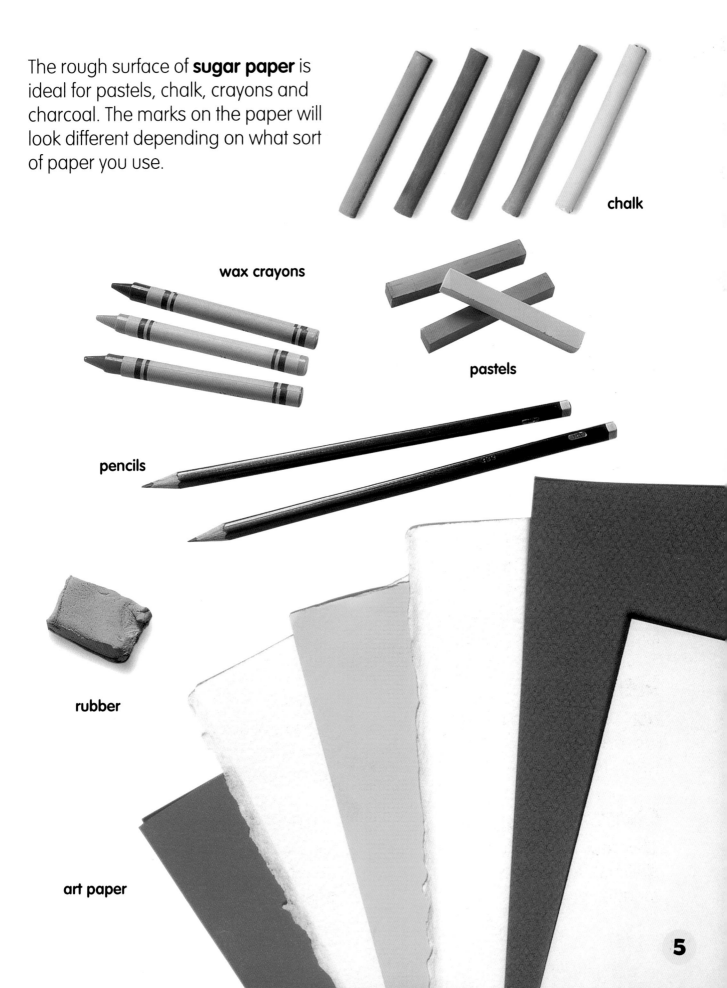

chalk

wax crayons

pastels

pencils

rubber

art paper

Get inspired!

You can get ideas for your drawing projects wherever you look. Carry a small sketchbook with you wherever you go so that you can jot down ideas and make quick, on-the-spot sketches. You can turn these into finished pictures later on.

When you find an interesting thing to draw, make a sketch and note its colour and **texture**. Texture is the surface of a thing – for example, it might be smooth, rough or bumpy.

Make an art collection

Collect interesting things to help you with your drawings. Create a mood board of things that you like, such as leaves, coloured scraps of paper, patterns, photos, stamps, labels and pictures from newspapers and magazines. Paste them into a scrapbook or file them away neatly in a large box. Empty cereal boxes make good art files, too.

Store your finished drawings safely in a **portfolio**. You can make one from card or thick paper.

1 You'll need two large pieces of thick cardboard, a strip of material, some strong tape or glue and some string or ribbon.

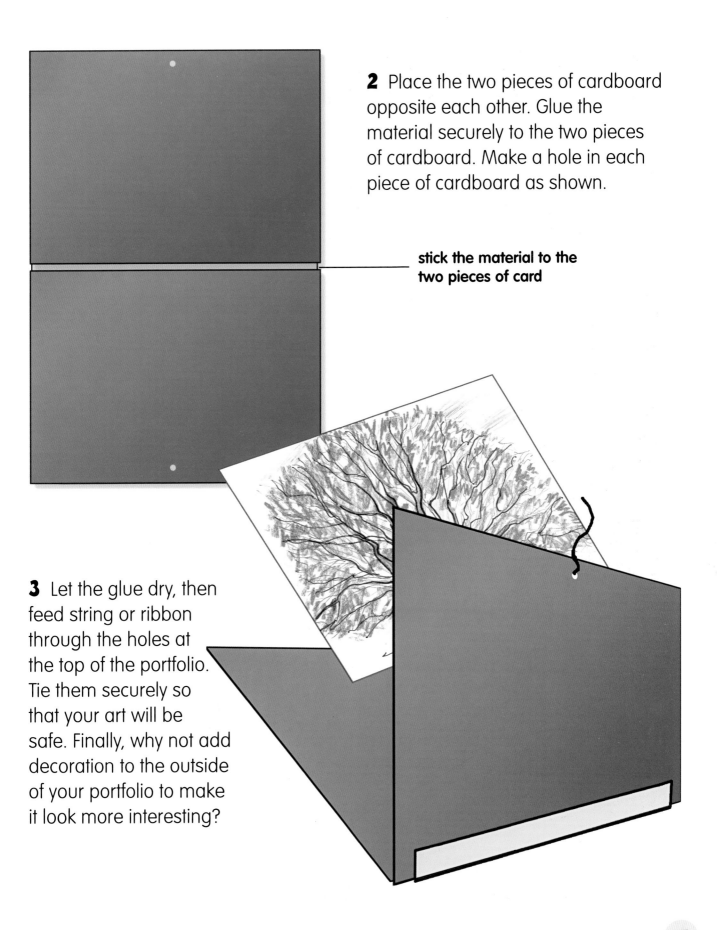

2 Place the two pieces of cardboard opposite each other. Glue the material securely to the two pieces of cardboard. Make a hole in each piece of cardboard as shown.

stick the material to the two pieces of card

3 Let the glue dry, then feed string or ribbon through the holes at the top of the portfolio. Tie them securely so that your art will be safe. Finally, why not add decoration to the outside of your portfolio to make it look more interesting?

Colour and shade

You can colour your drawing in solid blocks of colour – this makes bold, dramatic pictures, but it can look a bit flat. If you want your picture to look more three-dimensional, you need to add shade.

Hatching

This is how most artists add shade and texture to their drawings. You can make areas darker just by adding more lines. Try these techniques:

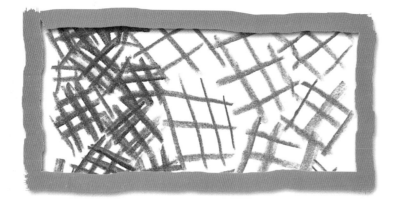

1 In cross hatching, you draw two sets of lines running across each other.

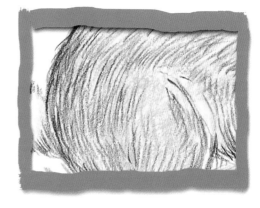

2 Curved hatching lines are good for making shapes look round.

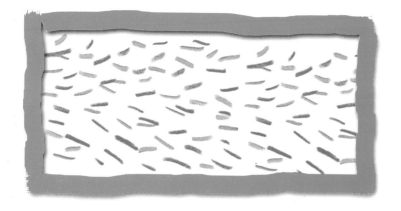

3 Use short lines for drawing fur or feathers. Experiment with pens and pencils.

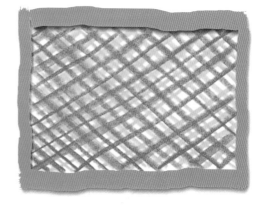

4 The more lines you draw, the darker the shade.

Scribble shading

Small scribbles are good for fast, energetic-looking sketches, such as this one of a guinea pig.

Smudging

Smudging soft pencil, pastel or charcoal lines gives a soft shading effect.

Making highlights

Use a rubber to remove bits of the shading and make **highlights**. This can create pools of light or make areas look shiny.

Dot shading

Closely drawn dots give soft shade to a picture. Try using more than one colour – from a distance, they seem to blend together.

Self-portrait

One of the best ways to learn how to sketch people's faces is to draw pictures of yourself. First sketch a quick self-portrait from memory on scrap paper.

Perfect portraits

Is your face round, oval, heart-shaped, square or long? If you can't tell, use a soft pencil or crayon and trace the shape of your face on a mirror – then you can look at the outline and tell what shape it is.

Before you start your self-portrait, think about your **features**. What shape are your eyes? Are your lips thin or full? Is your nose long or short?

Follow the steps on page 11. Look carefully at your reflection and draw a picture of your face. Think about the shading and texture.

Compare your finished self-portrait with the first sketch you did – you'll be amazed how much better your new drawing is!

Start by looking carefully at yourself in the mirror. Think about where your ears are in relation to your eyes and nose.

Follow these steps to help you get all your features in the right place:

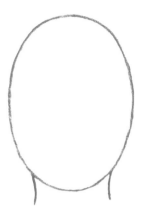

1 Use a soft pencil to sketch a faint egg shape for the **outline** of your face.

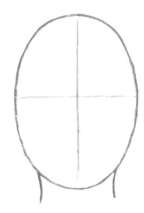

2 Draw a line down the middle of the face, and another one just above the centre from side to side.

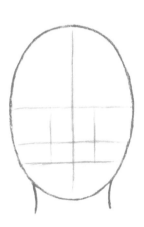

3 Now divide the lower half into two with another line from side to side. Then draw three more lines: one across and two up and down.

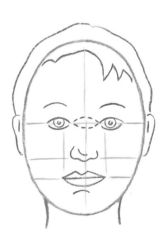

4 Use the lines as a guide to sketch in your features. Draw your eyes, leaving one eye width between them. Draw your mouth: start with the line between the lips, then add the upper and lower lips. Draw in the tip of your nose, but not the sides.

5 Add your ears, hair, eyelashes, eyebrows, chin and other details. Now you can add shading and colour with coloured pencils.

Drawing faces

Once you feel confident about drawing yourself, try drawing other people. Faces come in all shapes and sizes, and everyone's features are different. You can build up hundreds of different faces by making an Identikit set.

Identikit set

1 Draw four or five different face shapes, and divide them into sections.

2 Now cut lots of strips of paper, each the same width, as the sections in the face.

3 Draw different-shaped eyes on some of the strips, noses on others and mouths on the rest, all with different **expressions**.

4 Now mix and match the features on the different faces. You can cut out hairlines, moustaches and glasses, too.

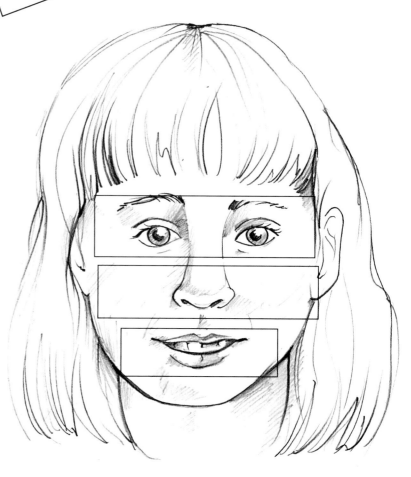

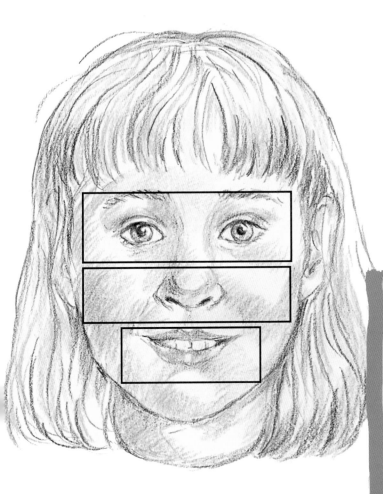

5 When you've created a face you like, trace or copy the outline and features onto another piece of paper. Use coloured pencils to turn it into a finished drawing.

EGG HEADS

It's not quite so easy to draw people's faces from the side, or from above or below! A hard-boiled egg can be a very useful part of your art kit.

1 Draw lines on the egg exactly as shown.

2 Draw in the features. Stick a blob of Plasticine on for the nose.

3 Using your egg-head as a model, practise drawing faces from different angles.

ART FILE

People don't smile all the time! Collect photos and newspaper cuttings of faces with different expressions, and practise drawing them.

Drawing people

The easiest way to draw figures is to think about the parts of the body as simple shapes. For example, think of the head as an egg, and the arms and legs as sausages!

1 Start with the head at the top of your paper. Draw an egg shape.

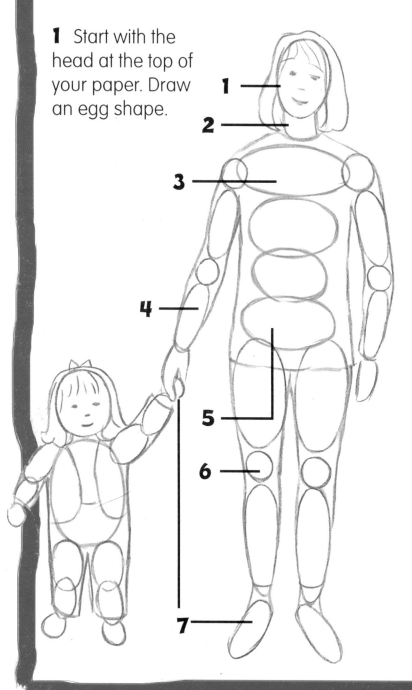

2 Add a short tube for the neck. It should be almost as wide as the head.

3 Now draw an egg shape for the top of the body.

4 Draw the arms as if they were two sausage shapes joined in the middle.

5 Draw the rest of the body using egg shapes and circles.

6 Draw the legs in the same way as the arms, but make them wider at the top.

7 Finally, add simple hand and feet shapes and draw the final outline to your figure.

Now draw your sausage and egg figures sitting, lying or crawling. Look at people in different poses or from different angles to get some ideas.

TRY THIS

If you draw these shapes roughly at first, you can add the details and colour in your figures later. Sketch lightly with a soft pencil. Rub out the original lines when your drawing is complete.

Make a poster

Find some photos of your favourite sports, movie or pop star, and draw him or her by building up from simple shapes.

Use different pens, pencils and crayons for your picture. What different effects can you create? Remember to use shading for the dark areas and leave highlights for the light areas.

SOCCER

Moving figures

How can you make figures look as if they are really moving? A number of simple techniques will help you bring your sketches to life.

Art in action

Choose a photograph of someone moving. Make a quick sketch of the figure, using loose strokes. Use your whole arm and not just your fingers and wrists. Try to look at the figure – not at what you are drawing!

Keep your pencil moving all the time, hardly lifting it from the paper. Draw sweeping lines that follow the direction of the motion. This will help convey the illusion of speed and movement, and make your figure look more realistic.

TIP

Take your sketchbook to an event where there will be lots of movement, for example a football match, ice skating or gymnastics. Make speedy sketches of the figures. You could also video an event from television. Freeze-frame the moments you are trying to capture.

Practise drawing action shots of sports people or dancers. The trick is not to draw detailed pictures of the people, just what they are doing.

Try using coloured pencils to make bold scribble drawings.

Finally, use your sketches to help you draw a finished picture.

TIP

Adding 'speed lines' really brings your action figures to life! Curved lines make your figures look as if they are twirling around. Straight lines make your figures look as if they are flashing past!

Perfect pets

Just as human figures can be made up of 'eggs and sausages' (page 14), you can draw great pictures of pets by combining simple shapes.

Cat

You can draw a cat from three simple circles.

1 Using a soft pencil, lightly sketch three circles, two for the body and one for the head. Make the head smaller than the body. Add the ears, front legs and the curl of the tail.

2 Use coloured pencils to complete the outline of the cat. You can now rub out any lines that you don't need.

3 Add details, such as eyes, whiskers, fur and markings.

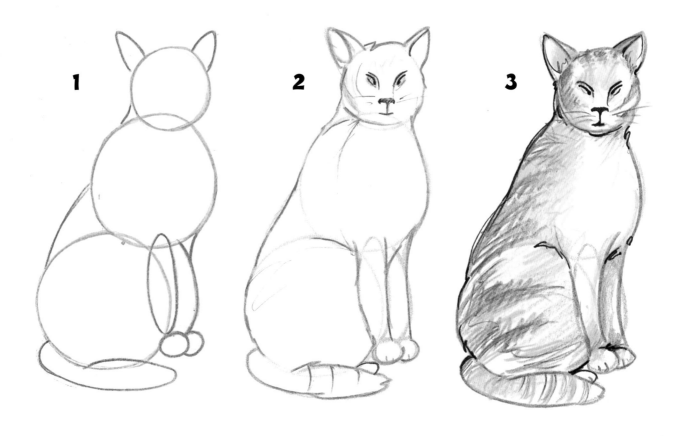

1 **2** **3**

Here are some other animals for you to sketch.

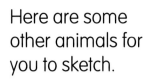

SCRAPBOOK

Collect pictures of as many animals as you can find. Save photos of your pets or of a pet that you would like to have. Collect pictures of your favourite animals on stamps, greetings cards, magazines or websites.

TIP

Try drawing different types of cats and dogs from photos – or from life, if they will sit still long enough! Remember that heads, tails, ears and fur are never the same, so look at them carefully before you begin.

Fur and feathers

Sketching the outline is the first step when drawing animals. To really bring your drawings to life, you need to add texture. One way to do this is to make different types of markings with coloured pencils.

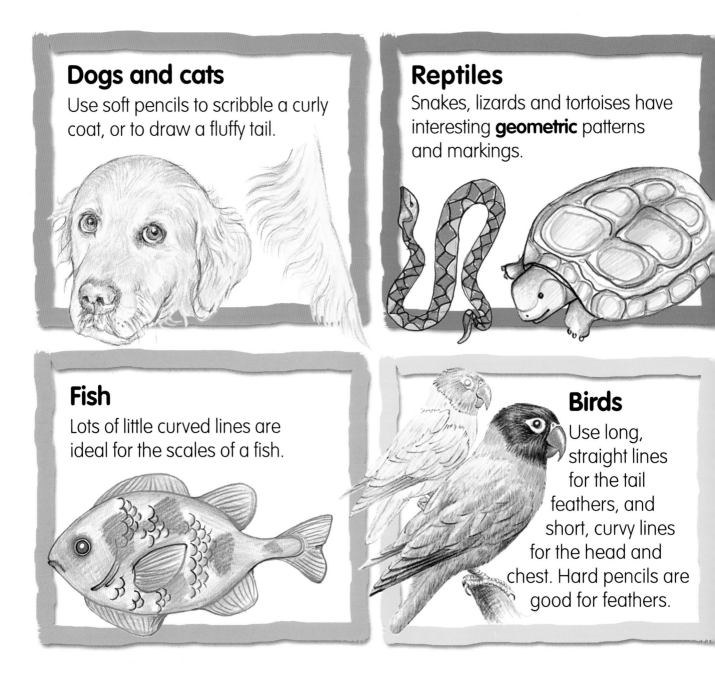

Dogs and cats
Use soft pencils to scribble a curly coat, or to draw a fluffy tail.

Reptiles
Snakes, lizards and tortoises have interesting **geometric** patterns and markings.

Fish
Lots of little curved lines are ideal for the scales of a fish.

Birds
Use long, straight lines for the tail feathers, and short, curvy lines for the head and chest. Hard pencils are good for feathers.

Experiment with different art materials to see which ones produce the most realistic effects for your animals.

Soft pencils or charcoal give a wider, softer effect, and are perfect for drawing fluffy animals.

Try drawing the same animal using different materials.

Hard pencils make thin, light lines – great for showing up this squirrel's fluffy tail.

Pens and felt tips make strong, black lines – the finer the point, the thinner the lines.

Drawing a view

When it comes to drawing a view, how do you decide which bits to put in, and which to leave out? Making a viewfinder can help you to decide.

Make a viewfinder

A viewfinder is a piece of card with a hole in the middle. If you make it out of two L-shaped pieces of card clipped together, you can change the shape to make a square or a rectangle.

1 Draw two L-shapes onto a piece of card.

2 Cut them out and use paperclips to hold the pieces together to make a rectangle.

1

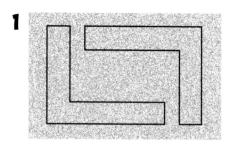

2

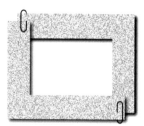

TIP

Silver or white pencils look good on black sugar paper. Use black pens or thick felt tips to draw **silhouettes** – such as a winter **landscape** or a sunset. Silhouettes are solid dark outlines on a lighter **background**. They look good against soft white tissue paper or silver backgrounds.

1

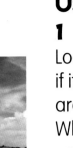

Using the finder

1 Hold the viewfinder in front of you. Look through the hole in the middle as if it were a camera lens. Move it around until you find the right view. What happens when you look at the same view **horizontally** and **vertically**?

2 When you have chosen your view, use your free hand to quickly sketch the main parts of the picture with a soft pencil (you can rub it out afterwards). This is your rough outline for the finished picture to indicate large areas, such as grass, sky or water. Sketch in the position of any buildings or trees.

3 When you have drawn the outlines, put the viewfinder away and finish the picture, putting in the details and using coloured pencils, chalks or pastels.

2

3

Looking at trees

As with all your drawings, it is important to look carefully at a tree before you try to draw it. Notice how the branches grow from one another, rather than all coming straight from the trunk.

There are a huge variety of tree shapes.

Some trees have long branches that reach out to the side.

Some trees are very tall and thin.

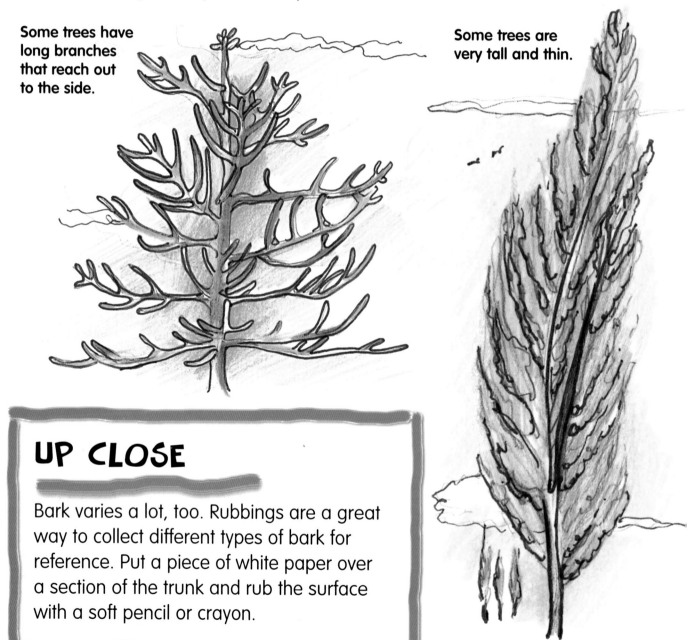

UP CLOSE

Bark varies a lot, too. Rubbings are a great way to collect different types of bark for reference. Put a piece of white paper over a section of the trunk and rub the surface with a soft pencil or crayon.

It can help to sketch the overall shape of a tree before you draw in the detail.
Try filling the whole piece of paper with your tree shape to make it really dramatic.

1 Lightly sketch in the trunk and the overall outline of the tree.

2 Draw the main branches, making them thinner at the ends.

3 Add fine lines for the smaller twigs, right up to the edge of the outline.

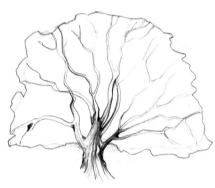

This is how the tree looks in winter, but deciduous trees change throughout the year. Leaves appear, change colour and fall; buds can be followed by blossom and berries. Try drawing a tree in different states.

Soft pencils or charcoal are ideal for drawing wintry trees. For a dramatic effect, use white chalk on black paper. Just colour the spaces around the tree, and in between the branches, to make dramatic silhouettes.

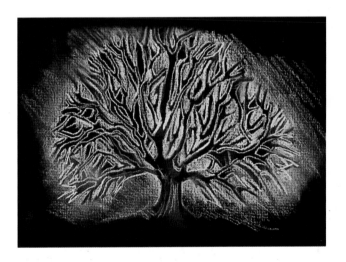

Cityscapes

A cityscape is a view of a city. Don't be put off by thinking that buildings are too complicated – the trick is to look at everything carefully and to build up the picture from patterns and shapes.

1 Decide what you are going to put into your picture. Are there any interesting buildings in your area? Use your viewfinder to help you decide which is the best view. You could use a view on a postcard or from a book.

2 Firstly, draw the outlines on a wide piece of paper. Look carefully at the buildings – are they wider than they are tall? Do the roofs slope steeply or are they shallow?

3 When you have done the outlines, sketch in the doors and windows. Check how big they are compared with the rest of the building.

4 Add the rest of the details, such as chimneys, turrets, porches, steps, stones, wood and brick patterns. Finish by adding colour, using white to create highlights for bright spots.

Build your own

To make a building look three-dimensional, you need to draw its side view as well as its front.

1 Draw the front of the building.

2 Draw in the sides, to make a **cube**.

3 Add a roof, door and windows

4 Shade the side of the house lightly – you could add a shadow to make it look realistic.

1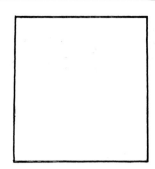

2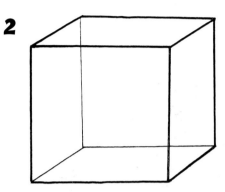

3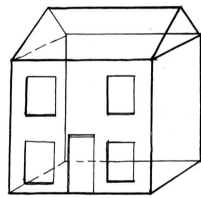

4

Using a grid

Drawing is about looking and copying exactly what you see. Sometimes our mind tricks us and we draw what we expect to see, not what is actually in front of us. Using a grid can help you get the **proportions** exactly right and can also help you to make your pictures larger or smaller.

1 Take a photo or magazine cutting, and trace the outline of the picture you want to copy onto tracing paper. Now divide your tracing into equal squares, using a ruler to help you.

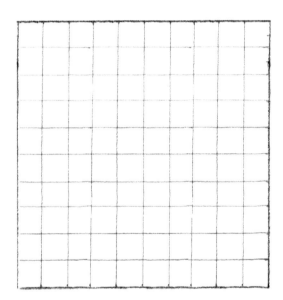

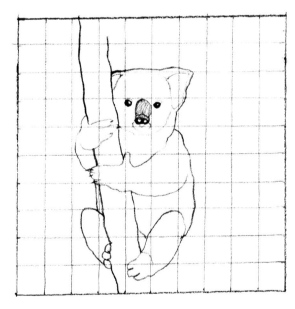

2 Take a sheet of paper and draw the same number of squares using a soft pencil. You can make the squares the same size as the ones on the tracing paper, or they can be smaller or bigger.

3 Copy the main outlines of the picture into each square one by one. Concentrate on each square at a time, rather than looking at the whole picture.

Upside-down drawing

Choose a picture from a magazine that you'd like to copy, and draw a grid over it. Make a separate grid on a sheet of white paper. Turn the original picture upside down. Now copy each square, including all the shading. Your finished picture will be much more accurate, because you are just copying areas of colour and shade, rather than trying to draw the details.

Using a piece of wallpaper lining, make a big poster of an animal for your wall. Use the grid technique with chalks or charcoals to fill in large areas quickly.

4 When the main outline is complete, rub out the guidelines and fill in the smaller details, using the photo as a guide.

Tools and materials for creating cartoons

Anyone can draw cartoons – the more you practise, the better you'll become! This section of the book has lots of ideas to help you improve your cartooning skills, along with exciting projects for you to try out.

Tools of the trade

All you really need is a pencil and plenty of paper, but it's also good to experiment with as many different materials as possible. HB or B pencils are ideal for first sketches – they rub out easily. You can go over the outlines in pen at the end.

Cartoon experiments!

Why not try using some other cartooning tools? For example, marker pens are great for drawing big, bold cartoons. You can use felt tips, poster paints and inks for making bold, colourful cartoons while coloured inks and **watercolours** are good for soft colours. Remember, if you use paint or ink, draw your outlines in waterproof pen or they will run when you start painting.

Paper

Use scrap paper for your rough ideas and smooth cartridge paper for your finished cartoons.

There are lots of different materials you can use to create cartoons. As you experiment with different pens, paints and pencils, you'll see they all create different effects.

wax crayons

pastels

pencils

felt tips

Drawing board

You need a hard surface to support your paper when you're drawing. Use a board positioned at a slight slope and keep the paper in place with masking tape or drawing pins. You need plenty of light when you are drawing, either from natural sunlight or a desk lamp.

Protect your cartoons

Artwork is easily damaged. Tape your best pictures to a piece of card and tape a piece of coloured paper over the top to protect it. Or make a portfolio (see pages 6–7).

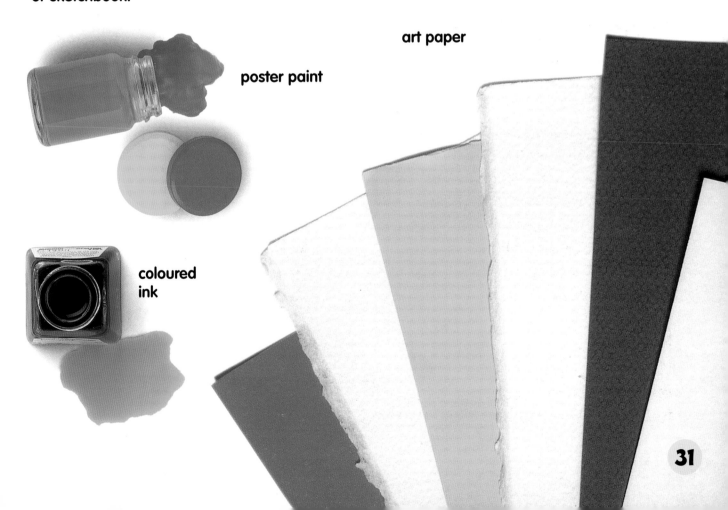

Keep your ideas in a notebook or sketchbook.

poster paint

coloured ink

art paper

Cartoon tips

Look for cartoon inspiration wherever you are: at home, at school, in the country or at the seaside. Draw a person, an animal or an object that you know well or use your imagination to create a fantasy character or monster.

What is a cartoon?

What makes cartoons different from other drawings? Think about your favourite cartoon characters from films, television, comics or picture books. Usually their features are exaggerated in some way to make them funny or scary.

'The Simpsons', created by Matt Groening, is known the world over.

ANIMAL MAGIC

Look carefully at different animals and make sketches of them. Real animals may not keep still for long, so look at books, magazines or on the Internet. You could also watch wildlife programmes on television. You can even use a microscope to look at tiny insects.

People pictures

Look carefully at your family, friends or favourite celebrity. Everyone has a unique feature that would make a great cartoon. Collect photos of people in different outfits, positions and poses. Look at them for ideas when you draw your cartoons.

MUM

DAD

Cool cartoons

You can get different effects depending on which tools you use. Use a black pen or felt tip to outline and shade your cartoons. Felt tips create bold outlines and flat colour. Coloured inks give a softer effect. Combine a black ink outline with pencils, coloured ink or watercolour.

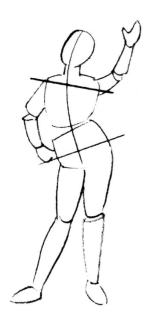

Cartoon figures

The easiest way to draw a cartoon figure is to sketch a simple outline first and then add the details. You can start by drawing stick figures or round people. Try the cartoon figure below.

Stick figures

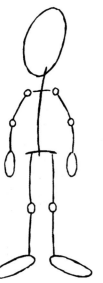

1 Draw a stick figure and add an oval head, hands and feet. Put small circles at the joints.

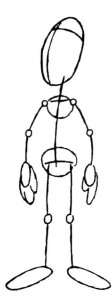

2 Build up the figure by adding an oval for the shoulders and one for the hips.

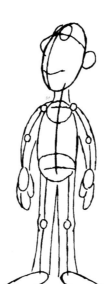

3 Draw the outline of the body and add the features of the face.

4 Add details for the face and clothing. Finish by filling in with colour.

34

TIP

You can use circles and ovals to make cartoon figures: stretched ovals make tall, skinny figures, while circles make plump people. Mix the two to create fat people with spindly legs.

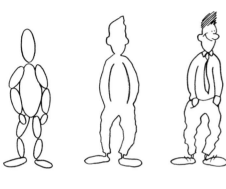

1 Draw the outline of your figure using circles and ovals.

2 Now add details to make them funny, such as hair, clothes and shoes.

Big and little

To draw a cartoon of somebody you know, look at them carefully. Are they tall or short? Fat or thin? Now exaggerate their most outstanding feature. Practise drawing from photographs.

Faces and features

Faces and expressions are important in cartoons. The face is the part that people look at, so they should say a lot about the character. You can make them funny, angry, sad – or just silly!

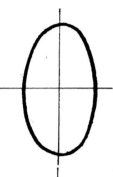

Head on

1 Draw an oval. Divide it into quarters.

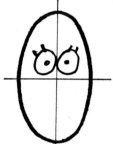

2 Put in the eyes just above the centre.

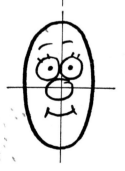

3 Add the nose on the centre line. Add the mouth under the nose.

4 Add hair, eyebrows and eyelashes. Make your faces happy, sad, grumpy, angry or frightened.

TIP

Try different face shapes: long and thin, short and fat! Fat heads have no neck. Thin heads look even skinnier on a long, thin neck.

Hair can make a big difference to your characters. Different styles can make characters look scruffy or glamorous, young or old.

If you are making someone you know into a cartoon, look at them carefully. What do you notice most about them? Do they have a long chin? A wide face? Ears that stick out? A big nose? Glasses? These are the features you can exaggerate to make a great cartoon.

Remember glasses and jewellery, too. Details bring cartoons to life.

TIP

Look at your reflection in the back of a large dessert spoon. With your face in the light against a dark background, draw what you see. Your face will be stretched and distorted. Copy this for an instant cartoon effect.

Dressing up

The way you dress your cartoon characters helps to bring them to life. Clothes and hats can help tell you where their owners live, what they do for a living or something about their personality.

Mix-and-match book

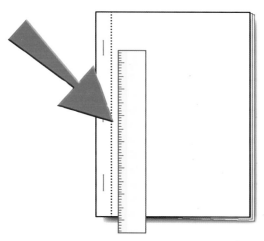

1 Staple 8 sheets of unlined paper together to make a book. Draw a **vertical** line 5mm from the spine.

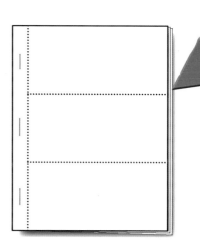

2 On the first page, using a ruler, divide the page into three equal horizontal sections.

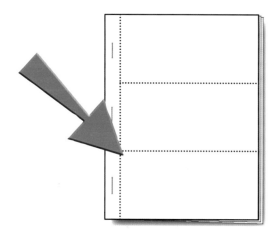

3 Ask an adult for help with this step. Cut along the horizontal lines as far as the vertical line, using scissors.

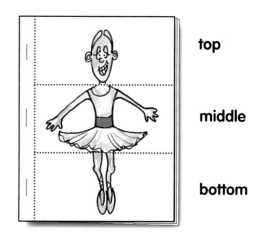

top

middle

bottom

4 Draw a cartoon character on the first page. Put the head and neck in the top third, the body in the middle and the legs and feet in the bottom.

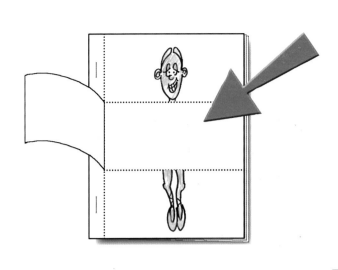

5 Flip back the middle section and mark where the neck and legs join the body on the next page. Use this as a guide for your next page and draw another character.

6 Repeat the steps above. Flip the sections back and forwards to make mixed-up cartoon characters!

On the move

Now you've created your cartoon characters, you need to make them move. Follow the hints and tips below to get them running, jumping and flying.

Action!

1 Begin with a simple stick figure.

2 Then add ovals and circles.

3 Now add clothes, colour and facial **expressions**.

4

Jumping

Running

Movement lines help to show which way something is moving – and how fast.

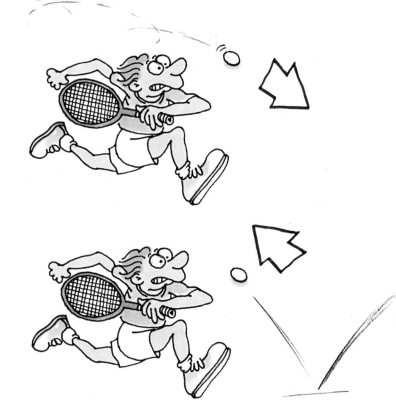

TIP

Movement lines also add extra action to your cartoon – just look at the pictures below. Adding double movement lines behind these figures makes them look more active.

Cartoon creatures

Before you start drawing cartoon animals, practise sketching real ones. Then try turning your sketches into cartoons.

Drawing animals

Have a look at the features and **personalities** of a variety of animals. A dog's ears can be droopy or perky, depending on whether it is happy or sad.

KOOKY ANIMALS

You can build up any kind of animal from simple shapes.

Animal shapes

1 Draw an outline of the head and body, using circles and ovals. Add the legs, feet and tail.

2 Rub out the guide lines you don't want in the final picture.

3 Use coloured pencils or pens to finish the drawing.

When you are confident about drawing animals, try stretching the body and limbs to make them taller and skinnier, or squash them for rounder, fatter, more comical cartoon creatures.

TRY THIS

Create a new animal star
Some animals have been turned into cartoons many times – especially bears and cats! Try to think of something more unusual and see what you can do with it. Will it be fierce or friendly? Clever or stupid? Fast or slow?

It's alive!

Cartoons can make anything come to life. Look around your bedroom, garden or classroom for inspiration. You could turn your whole street into cartoon characters. The windows of the buildings could be the eyes and the doors could be mouths!

Kitchen cartoons

Choose an object and get to know it well. Draw it so often, and from so many different angles, that it becomes as familiar as a friend.

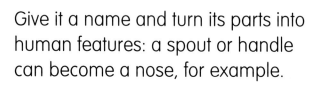

Give it a name and turn its parts into human features: a spout or handle can become a nose, for example.

Motor mouths

Give bikes, cars, scooters, skateboards, boats, trains and buses funny faces to bring them to life. Try to make the shapes match the expressions – for example, a car can be round, smiley and friendly, or long, low and aggressive, with a long radiator that looks like a mouthful of flashing teeth, and wicked eyes instead of headlights.

Scary monsters

People, animals, buildings or houses can all make scary cartoons – and that's before you start drawing the real monsters, such as vampires, werewolves and ghosts!

Everyone will recognize a vampire. How about making up your own monsters?

Wicked witches are usually ugly and have pointed noses, long chins and warts on their faces.

1

2

3

You can make ghosts as black silhouettes, or as white, cloudy shapes with a soft, black outline in the shape of a whirlwind.

MONSTER MIX UP

Try mixing parts of different animals into a new fantasy friend ...or **fiend**!

A question of size

Even tiny creatures can become terrifying if they grow to a huge size.

TRY THIS

Mythical monsters

Myths and **legends** are full of strange and scary creatures, such as dragons, werewolves and devils. Choose a mythical monster and turn it into a cartoon. Will yours be scary, friendly, or funny?

Set the scene

Once you've created a group of cartoon characters, it's fun to put them in different backgrounds. Use real life or invent a fantasy world – your background will be far more interesting than a blank piece of paper.

TIP

Always start by sketching your cartoon character in soft pencil first, and then add the background. Add **foreground** details last. When you are happy with the finished result, colour it in and go over the outlines in thick, black pen.

Where to get ideas

Flick through travel magazines, photos and books, or look around your house, street or school – which of these scenes suit your cartoon characters? Draw some simple backgrounds – choose a few details that show where it is meant to be.

Placing your character

Your character should appear to be part of the scene, not just stuck on top of it – make sure that there is some detail in front of your character, as well as behind.

Night or day?

Night-time backgrounds are great for a spooky atmosphere. Draw your character and buildings in black silhouette.

IN THE MOOD

Different skies set the mood, too. It's easy to fill the sky with snow or rain!

Comic capers

Now that you've learned how to draw amazing cartoon figures, you can put them in your own comic story. First, take a look at some of your favourite comics. You'll see that the pages are split into **frames** of different sizes and shapes.

Frames don't have to be square! Try circles, ovals and ones with jagged edges. You can draw the frames by hand so that they are not all straight lines or you can draw them neatly with a ruler. Comic strips look more exciting if parts of the picture break out of the frame.

Story lines

Your characters can 'talk' in speech and thought bubbles. You can put extra information in boxes at the top or bottom of the picture if you have left enough space. Speech bubbles are usually oval. Bubbles that look like clouds show a character's thoughts. Jagged bubbles show when someone is angry and shivery bubbles when they are scared.

Exclamation marks!

Exclamation marks are used a lot in comics. To show people shouting, use a thick black marker pen.

TIP

Speech and thought bubbles usually go in the top third of the picture, so draw your sketch in the bottom two-thirds.

Make a comic

Now that you've seen how it's done, why not try creating your own comic story with your own cast of funny, scary or silly characters? You could even make a whole comic book.

Lights, camera, action!

Making a comic strip is like making a film: you need a story, characters and a series of backgrounds. Start by thinking up a short, simple story with a beginning, a middle and an end. You could look through some joke books for a funny ending.

Stars of the show

What will your main character look like? Decide what sort of personality they have and think of a name. Try drawing them from lots of different angles to get them right. You'll also need friends and enemies for the main character to talk to. Try not to have more than three characters, otherwise readers may get confused.

YOUR CARTOON CHARACTER CAN DO ANYTHING!

Storyboarding

You're ready to make a storyboard. This is a rough sketch of each frame; it doesn't have to be perfect. Try to vary the pictures. Sometimes characters can be in the distance, sometimes you can show a close-up of their face and expression.

Comic frames

Once you are happy with your storyboard, turn it into a finished comic strip. Draw each box neatly, with a ruler and a pencil. Make sure you draw the frames big enough to fit all the details you want.

Finishing off

Copy your drawings from the storyboard and turn them into finished cartoons. First, draw the outlines in pencil.

Go over the outlines in black marker pen or felt tip. Colour the pictures with paint or felt tips. Your comic is complete!

Making movies

In an **animated** cartoon, thousands of pictures are shown at the rate of 24 pictures per second. This is too fast for our eyes, so we see a continual movement. If they were in an animated cartoon, these 12 pictures would appear on screen for just half a second!

1 2 3 4 5 6

7 8 9 10 11 12

Make a flick book

Make a simple flick book to see your cartoons really move! You will need a small, unlined notebook and a pen or pencil. Decide what you want to see animated – kicking a ball for instance. Think about what you do when you kick a ball – try it out and see what your arms and legs do.

1 On a scrap of paper, sketch about 20 stick figures. Change the position of the arms and legs slightly each time so that the figure really looks as if it is walking or kicking a ball.

2 Copy the first stick figure in the bottom right-hand corner of the first page of your notebook.

3 Draw the second figure in the same place on the bottom corner of the next page. Keep going until you have drawn all the figures.

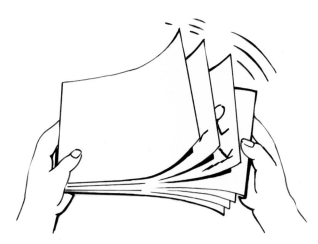

4 Bend the book slightly with your thumb at the edge and let the pages flick up. Your figure will appear to move! This is similar to how cartoon films are made.

Try drawing different types of movement. Ask a friend to do the movements for you to copy or draw from your own reflection.

TIP

Animators use 'key drawings' to help them work out a sequence of movements. If you want to draw someone running, jumping – or just drinking a cup of tea – draw the start, middle and end positions first. These are your 'key drawings' – all you need to do now is to draw the sequences in between.

Glossary

animation   images made to look as though they are moving by showing many frames per second

B   soft pencil; even softer ones are marked 2B, 3B and so on, up to 6B

background   the area of a picture behind the main object – for example, a field and distant hills

cartridge paper   very smooth, high-quality paper that is good for finished drawings

chalk   a stick of soft material used for making smudgy pictures

charcoal   a drawing tool made from charred wood

cube   a square, six-sided, three-dimensional shape

expression   the look on a person's face that shows that they are happy, sad, puzzled or angry etc

features   ears, nose, eyes and other parts of the face that make us all look different

fiend   an evil creature

foreground   area at the front of a picture

frames   boxes that make up a page in a comic book or graphic novel

HB   medium pencil; even harder pencils are marked 2H, 3H and so on, up to 6H

geometric   having a regular pattern of recognizable shapes

highlights   the brighter parts of a picture

horizontal   across a page, from side to side

landscape   a scene such as a country landscape, showing trees and hills, or an industrial landscape, showing factories and buildings

legends   stories about superhuman beings in the past

myths   traditional stories from various cultures that explain their history or beliefs

nib   the writing end of a pen

outline   the outer lines of a figure or object in your picture – usually you draw these first and add the details later

personality   the unique way each person behaves

portfolio   a case for storing and carrying your drawings

proportion   the relative size of one thing as compared to another

resist work   a form of printing in which you cover a raised surface with ink or paint and then press this down on a sheet of paper

shading   adding dark areas to a picture

silhouette   a picture that is done by drawing an outline and filling it in with one solid colour

sugar paper   a rough-textured paper that is good for chalk and charcoal drawings

texture   the surface of something – some paper has smooth texture, others have a rougher texture

vertical   up and down a page, from top to bottom

watercolours   paints that mix with water

Index

Notes for parents and teachers

The projects in this book can be used as home projects or as part of an art class. The ideas in the book offer children inspiration, but you should always encourage them to draw from their own imagination and first-hand observation, as well as from memory.

Sourcing ideas

All art projects should tap into the children's interests and be relevant to their lives and experiences. Some stimulating starting points might be the following: found objects, discussions about their family, friends and pets, hobbies, TV programmes or topical events. Encourage the children to gather their own ideas and references from books, magazines, comics, the Internet or CD-ROMs. Digital cameras can create reference material (such as pictures of landscapes, people, or animals) that can be used alongside the children's finished art work.

Give the children as many first-hand experiences as possible through visits to galleries and visually interesting places. Try to arrange contact with creative people.

Before introducing the projects on cartooning, show the children a variety of animated cartoons and movies, ranging from traditional and contemporary hand-drawn cartoons to clay-model and computer-generated animations. The children can also look at a range of comic books, from simple comics aimed at toddlers to graphic novels.

Other subjects can often be an ideal springboard for art or cartooning projects.

For example, children can collect reference material for a landscape picture during a geography field trip. They might make bark rubbings or collect leaves. Similarly, a story from Greek mythology could be retold in picture-strip form. Encourage the children to look at the way that picture-book illustrators have used cartoon strips to retell history, legends and stories from literature.

If you have access to a camcorder, ask the children to storyboard a simple animated cartoon sequence and record it frame by frame to see how well it works. Encourage them to think of music and sound effects to go with their cartoon, as well as ways of making instruments from everyday objects. Cartoon figures can also be created from modelling clay. These can be made into cartoons by using a video camera, moving the models slightly each time you record a frame.

Encourage the children to keep a sketchbook of their ideas and to collect other images and objects to help them develop their drawings and cartoons.

Evaluating work

Help the children to judge the originality and value of their work, to appreciate the different qualities in others' work and to value ways of working that are different from their own. Display all the children's work and encourage them to talk about it. What do they like best/ least about it? How would they do it differently next time?

Show the children examples of other artists'

work – how did they tackle the same subject and problems? Do the children like the work? If so, why? Or why not?

Discuss the use of different materials, such as felt tips, markers, inks and watercolours. Experiment with different effects.

Going further

Look at ways to develop projects – for example, many of the drawing ideas in this book could be adapted into paintings, collage and print-making. The cartoons could be adapted to make printed T-shirts, cards and badges, or characters for board games. You could use image-enhancing computer software and digital scanners to enhance, build up and juxtapose images in interesting ways.

At school, show the students how to set up a class art or cartoon gallery on the school website. Having their work displayed professionally will make them feel that their work is valued.